Kangaroo's Guide to Keeping Fit

Published in 2026 by Windmill Books,
an Imprint of Rosen Publishing
2544 Clinton St.
Buffalo, NY 14224

First published in Great Britain in 2022 by Hodder & Stoughton

Credits
Commissioning editor: Sarah Peutrill
Series editor: Lisa Edwards
Series Designer: Rachel Lawston

Cataloging-in-Publication Data

Names: Edwards, Lisa, author. | Roberts, Sian, illustrator.
Title: Kangaroo's guide to keeping fit / Lisa Edwards, illustrated by Sian Roberts.
Description: Buffalo, NY : Windmill Books, 2026. | Series: Healthy habits
Identifiers: ISBN 9781538399552 (pbk.) | ISBN 9781538399569 (library bound) | ISBN 9781538399576 (ebook)
Subjects: LCSH: Physical fitness--Juvenile literature. | Exercise--Physiological aspects--Juvenile literature. | Exercise--Juvenile literature. | Kangaroos--Juvenile literature.
Classification: LCC RA781.E393 2026 | DDC 613.7'1--dc23

Printed in the United States of America

CPSIA Compliance Information: Batch #CSWM26
For Further Information contact Rosen Publishing at 1-800-237-9932

Healthy Habits

Kangaroo's Guide to Keeping Fit

Lisa Edwards

Siân Roberts

WINDMILL BOOKS

Kangaroo lives in a group called a mob. The mob likes to move around in the mornings and evenings and rest during the day when the sun is hot.

Mornings are a good time for you to exercise, perhaps on the way to school or during playtime. Exercise makes your body stronger and healthier.

Kangaroo's baby brother is called a joey. He lives inside a pouch on his mommy's tummy. When he is six months old, he leaves the pouch to exercise.

It's fun to exercise outside.

When you exercise your breathing gets faster.

You need to breathe in lots of fresh air
to help your muscles work.

Kangaroo can't walk like you because she can't move her legs one at a time.

Instead, she pushes off the ground with her tail, then jumps with her legs.

You can walk as fast or as slow as you like, and even run if you want to. The faster you move, the faster your heart beats. It is pumping your blood to your muscles.

Kangaroo uses her large feet and powerful back legs to jump in the air. When she is older, she will be able to jump nearly 6 feet high and 30 feet forward!

Skipping and jumping are good for you too. Do you think you could jump as high as a kangaroo?

Kangaroo can move really fast, up to 44 miles per hour when she is grown up. That's faster than a racehorse!

If you want to go faster, you can ride a bike or a scooter. It's good exercise too! Just don't forget to wear a helmet, and make sure an adult is nearby.

Kangaroo can swim across a river. She keeps her head above the water to breathe and paddles with her legs. She uses her tail to push herself through the water.

Swimming uses all the muscles in your body. As you become stronger, you are safer in the water too. It's great fun to splash around!

Kangaroo can't sweat so she relaxes in the shade when it's hot.

Sometimes she licks her arms and paws to cool down!

You sweat water when you exercise so you need to drink lots to replace it. It's important to cool your body down after exercise, and to warm up beforehand.

Kangaroo is boxing with her baby brother. Male kangaroos train to box or wrestle when they are young, usually with other young males.

You can exercise with other people too, by playing a game with two or more people. It makes it more fun!

Playing a game where
you throw, catch, or hit a ball
with a bat can be very fun
with other people.

Thank goodness Kangaroo is
good at catching Koala!

Kangaroo sleeps during the day. She needs to rest her body so that her muscles can recover after all that jumping.

After lots of exercise, you will feel tired too. Make sure you get a good night's sleep so you can jump around like Kangaroo the very next day!

Kangaroo can't climb, but her cousin the tree kangaroo can! His arms are much stronger.

You can climb a tree too, but it's safer to use an indoor climbing wall or outdoor frame. Always make sure an adult is with you.

Kangaroo loves to hang out with her family - they eat and drink together, and jump around and rest together.

Exercising can make you feel happy and full of energy. Do you have a favorite sport or type of exercise that makes you feel good?

Kangaroo has been showing us how she keeps fit. How can you keep fit?

Exercise every day

Exercise in fresh air

Walk or run as much as you can

Jump, hop, and skip too!

Ride a bike or scooter

Go for a swim

Remember to drink lots of water

Exercise with other people

Have fun with a ball game

Climb to grow stronger

Exercise to feel good

Remember to rest

Glossary

Boxing male kangaroos use their short front legs to try and push each other over. This is called boxing.

Exercising moving your body around until you breathe quickly and your heart beats faster.

Heart a pump inside your chest that moves your blood around your body.

Joey a baby kangaroo. Baby koalas have the same name.

Mob the name given to a group of kangaroos.

Muscles the parts of your body that make it move. They are attached to your bones.

Racehorse a horse that is trained to run very quickly.

Wrestle kangaroo males try to pull or throw each other to the ground. This is called wrestling.

Let's talk about healthy habits...

The *Healthy Habits* series has been been written to help young children begin to understand how they can live healthy lives, both in their relationships with others and in their own bodies.

It provides a starting point for parents, caregivers, and teachers to discuss healthy ways of being in the world with little learners. The series involves a cast of animal characters who behave in healthy ways in their own habitats, relating their experiences to familiar, everyday scenarios for children.

Kangaroo's Guide to Keeping Fit

This story looks at all the ways you can make sure you are keeping your body fit and healthy.

The book aims to encourage a child's awareness of how moving their bodies can improve their overall health and the importance of exercise, hydration, and rest. It offers children a simple set of basic exercise and body-care ideas to help them maintain their health.

How to use the book:

The book is designed for adults to share with either an individual child, or a group of children, and as a starting point for discussion.

Choose a time when and the children are relaxed and have time to share the story.

Before reading the story:

- Spend time looking at the illustrations and talking about what the book might be about before reading it together. Ask the children to look at the details in each picture to see what all the creatures are doing – some of them are echoing the main themes in the background of the story.
- Encourage children to employ a "phonics-first" approach to tackling new words by sounding them out.

After reading the story:

- Talk about the story with the children. Ask them what their favorite ways of moving their bodies are: maybe games or sports; dancing, walking, or riding a bike. How does exercising make them feel?
- Ask the children why they think it is important to keep fit. How do they feel when they sit around for long periods of time? Do they feel full of energy or tired?
- Place the children into four groups and assign each group a different form of exercise. After a short group warm-up, ask half of each group to practice their exercise and tell the others how it makes their bodies feel. Ask the group to write down their findings.
- At the end of the session, with the whole class, discuss how the exercise types made them feel, demonstrating that they have similar effects, like increased heartbeat or breathing faster. Stress the importance of warming up the muscles, cooling down afterward, and drinking water to rehydrate.